"In the end what is a blurb but a set of words trying to convince you to read a different set of words. You should do that right now, open this book and read those other words inside this book which are better words than these words. Look anywhere inside & spy for yourself. The table of contents gives you: Where are the worms in my mouth brother in your mouth and Skinny Fisted Sons and A Poem to Pass the Time. Or open any poem by David Greenspan to dare career down an unsure tunnel, lulled and stricken by sudden gashes of light & by the yelps of an unfortunate fellow traveler, sleepy, riveted, and frightened all at once. 'call it a vulgar display / of friendship   a song of sorts / chanted with lipstick / in our blood ... & anxiety   an idea about / the fine hewed quality of mistakes" Open it now. You'll be grateful for the starling companions & shocked by the strange reflection in the passing glass.'"

— Christopher Janke, author of *The Thing Itself*

"Flush with grief, insistent in its longing, at times flashing with anger, the language of David Greenspan's poems—so exact, so exacting—propels the reader into all the open astonishment that the Ordinary affords us. What more could we ask of poetry than that?"

— Richard Deming, Director of
Creative Writing at *Yale University*

"David Greenspan's innovative poetry has us touching our jaw, knee, and elbow, a sensuous unzipping not of clothes but flesh. 'I was a person   silicate & dirt / detritus of human / waiting for the right weather'. Here is the poetry aimed at our thoughts placed into every muscle and how we manage the weight of being human as we bend, unbend, alive with these brilliant poems! I am grateful for this book!"

— CA Conrad, author of AMANDA PARADISE:
Resurrect Extinct Vibration

"In this visceral and powerful debut, David Greenspan exposes a world within the world we inhabit, one full of histories often left unspoken. But this is not a book simply about despair or grief; instead, Greenspan masterfully turns elegy into ode, a story of one still standing after a storm of 'inaccurate weather.' *One Person Holds So Much Silence* asks what it means to inhabit a body and what it means to live a life that unfolds in unexpected ways. It's a stunning collection that continues to open through each subsequent reading, a collection that I think about as I make my way through a fractured world that begins to make more sense because of these impressive and carefully wrought poems."

— Adam Clay, author of To Make Room for the Sea

"*One Person Holds So Much Silence* proves that despite our disconnection, the body is no remote thing. Greenspan's visceral and poignant poetry confronts us with the notion that in life as in death 'we may have no answers.' And yet, we can not look away from these poems that deeply consider all the questions carried by our bodies."

— Gloria Muñoz, author of Danzirly

"The poems in this raw collection edge their way around the human body, taking note of the strange items that find their ways *in*: drugs, flies, milk, honeyed tobacco, etc.—these are prayers for the relative body and object. The speaker is concerned with the eccentricity of nuanced somatic desire. Here is a speaker 'shaped from ground / fondled to birth / without blood or mother' who asks questions and answers them without finality, but with resolve, sweeping us into the bewilderment of what actually constitutes a living form."

— Bianca Stone, author of *The Möbius Strip Club of Grief*

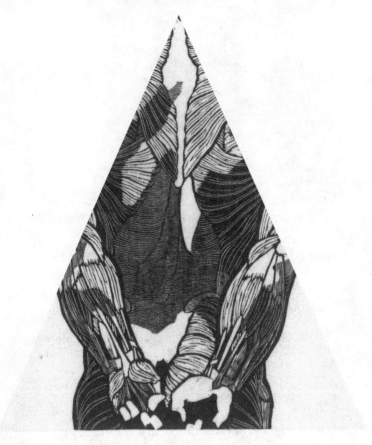

ONE PERSON HOLDS SO MUCH SILENCE

David Greenspan

INDEPENDENTLY PUBLISHED BY
DRIFTWOOD PRESS

Independently published by Driftwood Press
in the United States of America.

Managing Poetry Editor & Interviewer: Jerrod Schwarz
Poetry Editor: Andrew Hemmert
Cover Image: Reijer Stolk
Cover Design: Sally Franckowiak
Interior Design: Jerrod Schwarz & James McNulty
Copyeditor: Jerrod Schwarz
Fonts: Crimson, Merriweather, Bernard MT, & Manofa

First published March 8, 2022
ISBN-13: 978-1-949065-15-2

Please visit our website at www.driftwoodpress.net
or email us at editor@driftwoodpress.net.

Contents

We no longer
Use our bones. We are desperate we are fabulous
we are Possibly dead.

— *Sean Bonney*

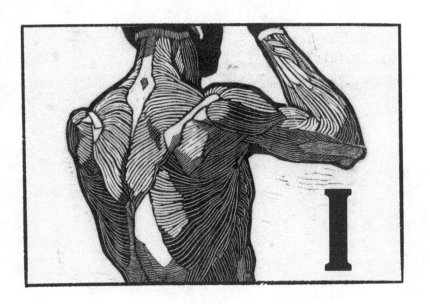

I

Poem for a god of my own understanding

Opening my palm on a fence
covered by frond rot   the cut
butterfat vulgar   bone in
all the wrong places   an embarrassment
of riches   I'll turn creak to croak
given time & patience   today
Florida covered in cuticle
mush warm   throat pink
bloated with Vicodin
no spit to speak of
how many times can I find myself
covered in honeysuckle
before I wise up
how many times can I pick out
my eyelashes before they stop
growing back   the doctor
sputters up lust small
tablets   can you tell me
why I was born
several hundred miles from
any ocean   opening
my knee on a mirror
watch sugary joy split
stutter   spill
effortless   this is how
we walk to the corner store
this is how we shake
from our bodies
a high bright whine

An incomplete history of

desire   in the beginning
a scratched throat   a throat
scratched   a mouth as empty
as Wyoming   a Wyoming
as empty as   //   hyssop
dipped in salt water   heated
in a throat   heat born
again as Wyoming   itself
dipped in fields of dried
salt water   spit from
a scratched   //   o
careful something or other
      wonderful throat
of Wyoming   o born again
heat   rope limbed
creature   fields of fields
of empty   o hyssop
left to dry along
a salted fold
of mouth   //   somewhere
this thing called pleasure
makes a white picket
      until we find
that place   that field
creatured   that house
throated   until then please
spit in & around my mouth

Some Days in April
after Rosemary Mayer

Pastel while observing
a quorum of fruit fly
do not disturb
leave milk if
income exceeds $17,000
per annum
alienation in violet
these unfrosting hours
some cloth
strung like self knowledge
is fetish
soft cloth
oxycodone the body
always another
hillside splayed
in museum weather
cream and all
pagan mouth

Skinny Fisted Sons

Splotched yellow teeth softishly
decaying, tobacco specked
like good livestock, fattened
ribbon winners. Oh yes let's
leer sour mash, gullet a drinking,
several drinkings, several hours of snarl
lipped in soy field. Blood
deer ticks the soil. No concern,
no knives. What flock would
deem to stop us? Come on then,
this the year of too much harvest.
Come on then, ethanol and animal,
spit against each other's fathers,
teeth against each other's grinnings.
These days out of order, we are
tinny with the heat of them.
Very little as interesting
as the weather. Decades of corn
kneed boys turning men, ash
elbowed along violet
smear of interstate, poppy crop
hidden in stomach. Tread on it
you poltergeist, you sympathizer, you
erosion. Tread on it and look at
all these magnificent ways we die.

The Body Itself Crude & Chanted

If like a fat radish
I am shaped from ground
fondled to birth
without blood or mother
then why

committing vomit
a slick feeling
follicle dragged
from my upper lip
if blood is god minor
waiting to sugar
to vein my body
& other failures
then what use
is gauze   tomorrow
a dulcet of plums
if they pulp
my throat   then why

a moment of slow
relief hiding
among limp stalked
fennel   if I live
outside vulgar Florida
across a porch
collateral
myself for milk money
& embarrassed
violence   then

if I am looking
spidered sick
in the mirror
then who is watching
this toothache
of self   this bruise
through curtains

Where are the worms in my mouth brother in your mouth

Q: Please state your name.

A: A release. A release of tension. A release of tension in the jaw.

Q: That's not a name.

A:

Q: Please state your relief.

A: Attention lathered upon, lateral against.

Q: Please list five references, personal or professional, who can speak to your bloat.

A: Self knowledge only goes so far. A faucet of eulogy.

Q: A jawbone of sorts.

A: See.

Q: Oh my / star. Chart / my progress towards / an absolute sense of / guillotine string.

A: All fish headed rumor.

Q: How are you doing threaded together so.

A: Anatomically correct diagram of a cat eye. Bolded red lines. Capillaries and caterpillars.

Q: Where were you.

A: Corneal abrasion, extraction.

Q: Stutter out your color.

A: Shivering.

Q: Two years is a long time.

A: Beneath my skin is a zipper. Beneath the zipper is more skin. Shapeless, without tuft of muscle, bone, organ.

Q: Endless reaches of lithium flavor.

A: I unskin myself and unzipper after.

Q: Water, in the right light, a food group.

A: I'm bored with the ocean.

Q: Can you address concerns over your inability to experience shame.

A: I was as much as anyone. Grafted and grifted the first time she found needles. Slouching toward death, both of us.

Q: Who was.

A: Others, of course others, but their names won't be repeated here or anywhere.

Q:

A: Not a mirror but a pane of glass.

Q:

A: A glass unspooled.

Q:

A: Puddles and thumbs.

Q: Can you add an indefinite article about the self.

A: Capital's throated maw. Its inertia, bulbous and confused, tonguing a genital.

Q: Dear selfish chemical, do not resuscitate.

Q: So here we are.

A: Mouth open and closed like a fish. Mineral clods its way out.

Q: Pulp spit and polish with care.

A: There is no blood without blood.

Poem for Florida

I find myself citrus pitched
and pulped in a gas station.
The cashier's fingers
like fat rain in my face
again again again
again. I've built something
closely resembling a life
of lemon bright distraction.
Pills and pills, limbs
and sour cigarettes, meat
at every meal. I read
poems written on apple skin
about the dead who stare
with red faced greed
at the dirt of children.
I pare the color
from my body again
again again again until
the dead come back
with berry stained hair.
Overdoses and tumors,
boxes of clementines,
they all come back
and go dancing. I watch
with a greased weight
in my chest. The sun rises
like today is any other day
and not the first time
every fear shows up
full of cough syrup. The sun

touches itself in the backyard
as the dead mosquito
around its ugly medicine. I sit
rat tail against dandelion stem,
bruised as ground fruit and
drinking from a hose.

Untitled Two

Collateral your nervous

unfinished mouth

hopeless then with vomit

for two thin cigarettes

Plagiarism of ritual

ordinary as rain

finds its essential tremor

Cleanliness a privilege

brutal gossip of the eyes

There are crayons everywhere

The first time my father cut himself

was an accident.
A seed had been planted
beneath his facial hair
and that isn't the right place
for a seed. The third time
my father cut himself
he posted a picture of it
on the internet. It was shared
over one hundred times
and a number of women
commented on his hands.
They're the ugliest I've ever seen,
one wrote. They're full of music,
one wrote. They're yellow
from years of smoking,
my father responded.
These women are now my mothers
and most days we sit
in front of the computer
looking at pictures of fingernails
and animals dressed
as people. I've been drawing
an anatomically correct human
kidney. I don't know
whether to include the pieces
of bark and apple I suspect
have worked their way inside
my father. I don't know
what to do dear ghost
when I wake covered

in a layer of salt. I don't know
what to do dear father,
dear insect. I don't know
what to do when I wake
and the hair has been pulled
from above my lips
and placed with great care
in a stranger's mouth.

Triptych for Our Ordinary Lives

One: The Living

Father a shape of glass
mother nicotine colored exposition
neither dog's metal leash
morning is violence   our bodies
matchstick   we swallow
last century's occult   today's vulgar
economy   spectacle of the dirt
nailed   an assembly of glands
rubber band welcomes eye
we were almost child   suckled bourbon ice
family is wound   in that pest house   we were
arterial   petite limbed
dear sibling   we married the dead

Two: The Years, Sometimes Many and Sometimes Few, Between

We are a collective of loosely associated ventures. An arrangement of worships. We are a brand but only in the sensing of emotion. You might say we are a rhizome of commodity forms, though we discourage you from expressing in this manner. It's called schizophrenia for a reason. Some of us lack bone, others lack parent, all lack water. Founded in 2004, we offer more substantial dividends than bonds yet come with a greater risk. We are an office in the right light, though you won't find our location by conducting a search. Try eating uncooked rice. We recommend starting with one handful and working your way to multiple. You can make a tax-deductible donation via bloodletting. Our executive and senior staff are some of the most awarded [redacted] in their fields. We are not accepting applications at this time. We will find you if you are a suitable match for an open position. Do not be alarmed if you hear reproduction from human resources. This is normal. Only use the approved break rooms. Their mirrors will reflect your most crumbled self with teeth once pale as ghosts.

Three: The Dead

Unzip our skin   pick the fat
goldenrod brushed
against what comes after
organ   we gloam
below Monday   there's rain
inside most bones
we lived with memory
we have no answers

An incomplete history of

airports   in the beginning
there was one daffodil
room   one large sky
     people spat & wondered
at their thumbs   milky
in their eyes   yellowed
in their teeth   people
twitched with urine desire
     walked towards limestone
& language   grain
& telephones & all
the rest   then fluorescent
lit concrete   pristine
with smiling attendant   people
talked   ate   slept   left
on the nine forty-five nonstop
to Dulles   with reasonably priced
tickets   time passed
     as it does   onion smell
piled up   standing in
line became a worship
     remove shoes for movable
altar   bathrooms
stayed bathrooms   remember
the awful prick & pressure
of cabin air   as we pluck
today's long-sleeved marrow

Palliative on Rooftop

We take a breath as the sun shakes
off its body. The roofing tar melted
during the day and sticks to our bare toes.
Our stomachs fat with apples
taken from a corner store. Matt decides to write
a philosophy of flinching. His American mouth
full of gray teeth. I sit, crumpled like an animal
wrapped in burlap, under the cistern.
Yes the air is indelible.
No we never find the cricket.
It's on the other side of the roof
and we aren't. We're selfish with our attention,
saved for each other's thighs. Sarah practices
giving Nikki a safety pin tattoo
in the ditch of her arm. Bits of glass
keep pigeons from bothering them. No one crowds
around the heating ducts. Our bodies lengthen
along this illegible night. Cars and rats hiss.
The sun wobbles back, catches Derek
reading a biography of painkillers.
How does it end? Not the biography.
With abscessed hands.
In Florida of all places,
home to countless endings of its own.
With clonidine and gabapentin
prescribed off label. We learn to hush
our more plumed desires. Learn the difference
between interstitial and all other suffering. We are
rich in gauze, whole tablespoons of blood

between our feet and hair. Piles of browned
fruit to eat each morning. We swallow
spidered lemon seed, sour pollen,
anything fit to be consumed. Dull to our throats,
all unfolding skin. We stay away
from mirrors and windows. Look
how helpless the bramble, the half-buried
palm. How helpless the word before
the word belief. At night we lie
on the sidewalk with cats,
watch their chests rise and fall
in time with ours. I place
a penny beneath my tongue.

Other Noise

Crude sibling of dirt
flinched
over shrill ocean
we pick at cuticle
porcelain source of data
always already speaking
collective pronouns
hum in the water
this former sidewalk
let's hold hands without
punctuation
our translation of flora
some bruise threaded
with delicate red stitching
labor unspecified
a syntax of pores
pathological in newsprint
cough a gallon of milk
a gloaming tomato
pockmarked emotion
stutter what is hungry

Nothing dreamy but the dream itself
aleatory on a pillow
pear shaped organs
ideological in nature
no such thing as success
whittle our chest to lesser failure
Greek myths at noon

rewrite them for today's audience
remember children
bright spread of what is possible
heat lisping off concrete
pedal the bike
hairless limbs sun shuffled
round words like quarters
two buy an ice cream
four buy a squirt gun
our unbuying in aisles
find the vetch
the dehydrated lavender
burn them
ring around their after

What folded hell is that
what coin placed where after who
what blood
our mouth apple tree ripe then spoiled
before one word leaves
lies contain truth like bones
contain surgical plates
don't start with semiotics
we've already shown our resin filled tooth
already dyed our hair
already counted the steps from gas station to porch
we don't have much
another lie
our hands full of cups themselves
full of sparkling
paint thinner
all these lonely crosses

Let's talk about the rattail
nervous twitch
skittish by training
rather than chemical
we made a self
a fugitive choice
mirror of ache
applause for our shared
arch of we don't want to feel like this
what rat
we've never seen any such creature
it's too hot to sweep
to bloom
memory an untruth
rain an unweather
worms brackish on the sidewalk
unspool with us

Body by Adderall

What do you know about nostalgia?
I can't figure it out. Maybe
it has to do with how we didn't talk
about daffodil, bone marrow, our parents
& how they would eventually die & we wouldn't
know what to do with our hands. Remember
when we snuck out of class & smoked cigarettes
& how your hair felt stretched tight
around my palm? Let's do that
with our hands. Let's pick stained grass
& feed it to each other. My stomach won't stop
growing. I mean growling. Did you know grass
is low calorie? Let's slice an apple
& watch it grow bruised. Let's slice an apple
& watch the air grow thick with flies.
What can you tell me about the years we spent
in basements? I remember the mice
& is that nostalgia? The smell of damp
wallpaper on my hands. The smell
of everything covered in a layer of dirt
& almost the same but a picture
moved, a water bottle spilled on your bed.
I'm wishing really wishing to be bone & water
but my skin has a zipper. Let me say it quickly
& briefly my skin has a zipper. Most days
I pick, pick, pick & is that nostalgia?
With hands sticky & red I raise
a glass of milk. One day we're going to die
& isn't that alone enough of a reason
to sit here & watch our nails grow?

An incomplete history of

pharmacies   before
sorted capsules   white
smile & the rattle of   *oh*
you know   one at each meal
     before supplements
& nicotine   nothing like a wrist
syringed   crisis of warm
piss down leg   before the first
blockbuster pharmaceutical
     handed out with military
disinterest   dead siblings still
years away   before
walls   brick plastered & boasting
ads for cough drops   medicinal
wines   tinctures   rejuvenation of body
& spirit   before morphine
jab   apathy from stomach
to rotten toe   ether cloth & your own
appropriated surgery
     before this there were the fat pads
of our fingers   taking up space
     warbled as horse muscle   a kind of
dissenting relief   things weren't better
just different   we sat in dirt   placed nettle
along our gums   let saliva
fall where it would   we've only ever
lived in half measures   only ever
drowned in bath water

**I don't like to sing about boxing
but I hope you'll understand**

A Kansas warm sun
shower & brown
baked whip of grass
& field standing
slender false foxglove
still. I'm sad enough
to put real thought
into how I'd kill myself
there, surrounded
by sweat & gnat
& grain feral sky,
but not sad enough
to do it. Dirt as blood
opens itself, seed
as bone or otherwise
gorged soft filament
all around. I'll call
a field rotten, another
field awe. Let's flip
for which is which.
For once you're right:
the broomcorn rotten,
the soybean awe. I'll spit
where & when I please,
mouth full to bursting
with Kodiak mixed loam.
Don't answer that call.
Don't answer that call.
I take safety white pills
because they keep me

at an acceptable level
of sad, somewhere
between fresh bread
smell & boxcar. Please
bloom now bloom plum
into anything
(please). The clouds
are jaundiced. They open
their throats & sing
shiny as a toy. Don't
mistake this for anything
other than what it is.
A shorter version of this
poem would read:
"Say boxing / say thank
you / say sadness yellow,
tin as wind chimes."

We the Dead Balk

We clot each other, bandage with fingers. Flutter at a softness of carefully darned socks. Let's all of us shawl, soft boil eggs, crush thistle. Dig feet into the apologizing remains. Should we set fire to what might burn. An obscure flag, a petrodollar. Describe their texture of smoke. What do we think when we hear sensual. A feeling of hands along other hands, water along filament. How much more can we syllogism. All ash is tactile. Lungs are ash. Therefore lungs are tactile. Blushed over skin to prevent infection. O insect sibling, the possibilities of glancing are legion. Our eyes affordable enough for anyone.

Our oldest friend nicotine. Sugared pinch of leaf with all sorts of incendiary. Braided against dissolving gums. A fresh & vacant space we name mouth, name teething. Afternoons when menthol splays the air, when our bodies husk themselves inappropriate, when even the strays complain. We question a logic of consumption. Bloated chemical edges out argument. Register the beggars, marvel at their fishhook. No more than several members of their family have asked for death. If we twine them, who will hear our assurances, our vague exuberance.

Our body has not found a destination & will be declared
stateless unless claimed before [   ]

We laugh like rodents wet with puncture wound, like hoarding months of nutritionally dense paste beneath cedar shavings. We cackle & swoon. Remember etymologies. Vowel of someone walking in a rhetoric sharper than our own. Reenactment of knowledge. When were we rats. Before scientists learned mischief, before we learned conventional violence. A buying & selling of socks. Table salt venture, no talcum to be found. Harvest on margin, we squeak, commission an estrangement of air. We will illustrate this failed animal.

The anatomy of household objects

We work out our salvation like any muscle
sure there's fear and trembling   burnt plastic
moments of panic   frustrated gods in the yard
snapping the ever so soft neck of our fennel
mostly the cat jumps and curls
around your arm   you lift her again and again
she paws you in pleasure or something close to pleasure
have you noticed how the fire extinguisher makes the room pop
do you remember that game with a parachute
we played in grade school   what about
feeling a fork-tined something
bulkier than sadness   remember your hands
when we mapped the anatomy of household objects
ice cube trays   garbage bags   pillow cases
cat litter   windows and mugs   the space beneath
couches   keyholes   sinks filled with hair
it was wonderful   the mapping   a hollow jawed
astonishment building and building until you were sure
your tongue was a cedar scented animal
but it was only your tongue   ordinary in every way
fat and warm as tap water

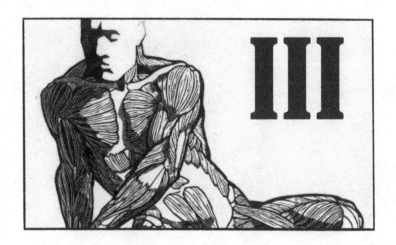

A Poem to Pass the Time

With lipstick on our teeth
with hands red & swollen
rich in soil nutrient   what a travesty
their daily mistreatment
covered in blemish
a century of decomposition
equals one foot of gossamer
call it our body without organ
not a straitjacket in sight
it was quiet when I found
dead hair in my bed   maybe
today I'll leave the house
enter a world of small violence
rain & restless legs
no umbrella   anyway I lied
it's a conversational tactic
I wanted to see
what an economy was
besides blood & equation
surplus value > cuticle mush
soft fur   softest fur
this side of the mulberry root   a rabbit
slant & eyelashed   one leg crooked
fur unspoiled gray   its thoughts
histamine   its body
solvent with tablespoons of blood
I'd like to be more than strangers
with this rabbit   what use is a landscape
without hair   a landscape meatless

pitied   my brush strokes
canvas movement   breath
through salted teeth   who said
I was a person   silicate & dirt
detritus of human
waiting for the right weather
where might I find a mannequin
to practice this self
loathing   a language
invented from the feather of lungs
if writing is dispossessed thinking
what is writing freed from thought
a perverse inventory   the kindness
of questions   the poem isn't very kind
my penmanship makes the whole world
nervous as a junkie on the third day
of withdrawal   burning crayons
for warmth   the neighbor downstairs
uses the bathroom   brews coffee
cinches a tie   sucks his teeth
a litany of the everyday
fidget in this river   yelling
doesn't get you noticed
speak stilted
carry a big clod of dirt
hide it in your cheek
blood on our lips
lipstick in our blood
we're laughing in an office
call it a vulgar display
of friendship   a song of sorts

chanted with lipstick
in our blood   it's wet
rub like a skittering oil
pockmarked patches of snow
our faces lit with communal emotion
an attempt at sadness
the sassafras bush
fearless & poor in leaves
tells me about rain
German pagans say in violence
we find chalk & circle
I'll stand against a wall
hand me a blindfold   from here
you can smell my yellow breath
hard yellow cocaine
no blinking
pause for nicotine
what astonishment
aluminum in my lungs   I guess my entire body
wants to scream   say please
say one person holds so much
silence   eyelashes pinioned
have you ever stared at your eyes
without a crown of lashes
think dog bones   burning rubber
promised a yard of swimming pools
I was never a man of my word
here's what I have   rats & their tails
laugh at a frequency higher than people
can hear   culpability of language
a rush of pencil on paper

number two & standardized
medication   smell of fresh industrial
morning   tall glass of what do you know
anyway   my material diagnosis
barely make it through the day
without sticking a needle in the top of my hand
I look balder than I feel
like a hardboiled egg   a quick mouth
a seasick ache   I was never
mentally ill just unfit for production
pessimism of the spirit
the feeling of a twenty-dollar bill
slid firmly between teeth
in a house with family
I hid in the bathroom
my cousin Emma talked about overdosing
felt it in my nails
this ellipsis   in my trashcan
mouse blood
shit & dried rain
so endless on our walks
behind my knees isn't much of anything
to worry about   is someone singing
no cigarettes until you clear your plate
oh yes they're singing
before I was a teenager
I took three Vicodin from Juliana's aunt
took codeine from a friend
I saw Georgia that night
she said I looked pale
& sick   reeked of eggshell

& anxiety   an idea about
the fine hewed quality of mistakes
how to commune without talking or eye contact
a matter of convenience   these are questions
with simple answers   where is the drain
how do I stop screaming
my tobacco honeyed mouth
who is watching   who is reading
a book about my father   I was most comfortable
when he wasn't watching
white gloved precision
he anesthetized our dog
beneath a pignut hickory sky
I was a child   I wanted to be
nothing   became a pile of silt
wet choked breath   sugary
go to the fields   the New England woods
eat what I find
I don't want to eat mice
fingers greasy from scooping
soft organs of walnuts
fat rain like a blanket
I can't understand anything
unless it's wet with metaphor
greased skin   primitive throat
homely motor of exploit
I'll stand still after
the body's inaccurate weather

SHADES OF UNCERTAINTY
A Conversation with David Greenspan & Jerrod Schwarz

Let me start by saying how wonderful it's been to prepare for this interview, David! Each re-read of these poems is as impactful as the last, and I am excited to discuss all that this collection has to offer. This is a multifaceted and complex set of poems, so I wanted to start off by delving into one of the unifying elements in the book: the body. Nearly every poem in One Person Holds So Much Silence investigates the human body in some way, both as an intimate aspect of personhood and a physical render of traumatic, cold truths. When you were initially writing these poems, what felt important to communicate about the body?

Thanks, Jerrod, and I'll start by saying what a great question. It's gratifying to hear my poems resonate with other people, move them, do anything publicly. You're a poet and can identify with the weird feeling of people reading your work. It's wonderful, even necessary in a way, but weird nonetheless. Okay, so, the body. It's hard to not be obsessed with this thing that is us, but is also incredibly alien to us. I don't want to fall into any sort of mind/body divide—we are our mind and body and the messy, indefinable between—but I'm often left with the sense that this thing that moves me around isn't me. Then there's how the body mediates our experiences. It's kind of impossible to get around that. Even when writing about something fully external, a tree or object or whatever, it's processed and becomes known to me, real to me, through my body's understanding of it. In a way it becomes part of my body, which leads to a really interesting blurring between human and nature, human and commodity, subject and object, internal and external. Even between two bodies. This all gets at how the body records. Sometimes it records something beautiful and energizing. Sometimes it records a traumatic, cold truth. So, in a sense, our bodies serve mainly as receptacles for experience and recording and all the affective tension these bring with them. That's kind of wild to think about. I realize that's a bunch of stuff rather than a single idea, but that's maybe the best way to talk about the body. It's unfolding, changing, always working on external stimuli and being worked on.

That's a great way of framing the relationship to a body and its surroundings: as recordkeeping. If we extrapolate that framework out, we can start to think of different artforms as different methods of recording experiences. What can poetry 'record' that other artforms cannot? Or, perhaps phrased in a less sanctioned way, what is poetry good at detecting?

Poetry seems good at detecting/recording shades of uncertainty, multiplicity, expansiveness. All art does this to a degree – what are abstract expressionist paintings if not expansive? Poetry is uniquely equipped to record and explore this kind of multiplicity—maybe we should call it ambivalence—given its basis in language. I'm thinking of semiotics and the strain between sign, signifier, and signified. This occurs in the meaning and making of art, but it's easiest for me, and I'd guess others, to understand and experience in language. We use language all day. It's the first layer of almost everything we do. Then poetry enters and kind of torques up language's expressive quality, that strain and tension, and it's just...complicated and disordered and wonderful. I think this is true even in poetry that isn't explicitly concerned with uncertainty. Then there's how poets love the unexpected word, phrase, line, image. This casts new meaning on the language that's come before and changes the reader's understanding of language still to come. So maybe another, simpler, way of saying all this is that poetry works so much in surprise and surprise is well suited to recording itself. We remember the unexpected more than the mundane (perhaps to our collective determent). I'm also obsessed with the idea of uncertainty in my writing, so I might just be off on a personal tangent here.

If I could flip this question back to you—I read WHAT THE BARN CAN'T KILL recently and think it presents an interesting example of poetry's ability to detect/record. It does this in a strange way though given that it's erasure. This is recording via subtraction, which is kind of wild to think about. It also blends in visual art, so that complicates matters. Finally, it moves within arenas of incredible violence, so there's this shadow/recording of menace present. I don't know where I'm going with all this, but I'd love to hear what the process of making erasures and using visuals in that project was like. How did it affect poetry's detection/recording abilities?

Thank you so much for this generous reading of my work! Erasure poetry is so many things to so many poets (Mary Ruefle likens it to archeology, I believe). In terms of my own personal definition, I would say that, at its most basic and revelatory, erasure poetry reframes text as a conversation. Its both serendipitous and horrible, but I got to spend a lot of time in graduate school thinking about redaction poetry and the many political texts that came out of the Trump presidency. This had a profound impact on my idea of record-keeping, as it became inseparable from a view of poetry as communal and intersectional; I think often about jayy dodd's erasure of Trump's inaugural poem and how that redaction actually stitched so many different groups of people into one poem. I'm going to throw the question back to you (last time, I promise) and investigate the inverse: what does poetry look like when it is only concerned with the present or future? Have you ever noticed yourself writing a poem that feels very insular, and what did that look like?

Mary Ruefle is the champion of erasure poetry, isn't she? So good. I'm interested in the idea of erasure poetry as communal and intersectional. It is, but in a counterintuitive way. What I mean is it's built by removing someone else's thoughts, memories, emotions, pain. Things get even more complicated when the text being erased is political (thinking about the direct/representational nature of politics). I have yet to dabble in erasure, so I fear I'm the kid watching a basketball game and just marveling over people dribbling and flying and dunking. To answer your question, I think my poetry is inherently concerned with the past via present and future. It's kind of impossible for me to not bring all my past experiences, including reading experiences, to the poem in progress. Staying in that molasses of past gets boring at best and masturbatory at worst. The challenge becomes, or one challenge anyway, how to translate the past into something new through the poem at hand. There's also the unbridled optimism of writing the future into a poem. It isn't necessarily that everything will be great, or even okay, but that there *is* a future and I have the opportunity to explore it in the poem. As far as insular writing, I worry all my poems are that! I tend to get caught up in focus, language, syntax, diction, whatever and go all in on that element. Part of my tinkering/revision process is balancing that against other directions I want the poem to move toward.

Formally, the verse here is economic and taught, with many poems comprised of short lines or existing in wide swaths of blank space. How organic or shaped is line length and visual language in your writing process? What aspects of visual form are you most concerned with in your writing?

I like to try and let each line hold its own meaning independent of the larger poem's meaning(s). What is a specific line saying or doing when freed from the context of what comes before and after? Does it make sense on its own? Does it make multiple types of sense (emotional, logical/rhetorical, sonic)? Part of this is line length, word length, blank space, even the letters themselves and the punctuation used. These elements are endlessly fascinating to me. Then there's how a given line interacts with its neighbors, how a stanza does the same. I guess this is a long way of saying the visual language of my poems (great way to describe it, by the way) is totally *not* organic. I tinker with all of the above far too much. I worry sometimes it hurts the poem. Am I sacrificing something larger like meaning or reader accessibility for individual line style?

I feel that anxiety as well, that my control of the poem overshadows the honesty. That being said, I think your poems absolutely sizzle here and never feel overwrought. This is certainly a poem-by-poem question, but I'd be interested to know what your poems look like before the tinkering. What does an absolute first draft look like?

Thank you. It's always good to get confirmation that I'm not alone in my worries and that I'm not tinkering a poem to emotional death. My first drafts look like trash! I say that tongue in cheek, but also quite literally. My lines are much longer. Many lines and ideas are in prose. They're in different orders. There are a lot of brackets and XXXXs as placeholders until I find the right word or phrase. They're really all over the place. It's a cliché to say, but my first drafts are really just that—first iterations. I've been in workshops for the past three and a half years, so that's also had a huge effect on my drafts. Having the pressure of a deadline helps, maybe more than anything else I've found, to get words on the page. It's not entirely honest to call this pressure. It is pressure in a sense, but it's also a great freedom to be messy during the drafting process. Also, whoever I'm reading at the time comes through in my first drafts. Sometimes formally (line length, enjambment, stanza patterns, white space) and sometimes in a poem's content.

One Person Holds So Much Silence contains raw, intimate portrayals of self-harm and suicidal ideation. However, your poetry does not fabricate easy answers to these issues, stating "I don't know / what to do dear father, / dear insect." This is a heartbreaking but admirable aspect of the collection: seeing how each poem contends with certainty vs. honesty, watching it clamor toward something painful on purpose. What advice would you give to other poets writing about similar material? On a larger scale, how has poetry helped you process or understand personal traumas?

I've written like five answers to this question, and they all sounded hollow and forced. I think the best thing I can say, and the truest, is that life is so completely messy and uncertain and painful that portraying it as anything different in my poems feels wrong. It even feels actively harmful. That's not advice, but it's something important to remember while writing. I say that as much for myself as anyone else. To answer the second part of your question, I'm not sure poetry has helped me process or understand personal trauma. The world is a pretty horrible place. It's also all we have. People can be pretty horrible. They can also be kind and generous and encouraging. Certainly poetry has helped me acknowledge and name traumas both personal and collective. I'm not sure we do ever really process and understand them, though. My therapist would probably disagree with that, but that's why she's a therapist and not the one in therapy.

This is a beautiful response and one I wish more young poets could hear: that writing about trauma is not always the same as healing it. I also agree with your statement that attempting to cover up the pain and messiness of life can be actively harmful. Are there any poems or poets you return to that have exemplified this kind of purposeful, messy honesty?

Too many! Anyone I list here is only a small part of a much longer list. To start, though, I'd say Sean Bonney, Bhanu Kapil, Cynthia Cruz, Larry Levis, John Murillo, and Anis Mojgani. Each of these poets have their own version of purposeful, messy honesty. Sean Bonney is probably closest in style to my own writing (at least that's my hope). He also writes in a more straightforward manner about things like self harm and addiction. I tend to dress these up in figurative language, while Bonney would write, "I'm withdrawing from opiates and want to die." I admire that more than I can say.

Bhanu Kapil is fearless in form and subject matter. Her book length projects always amaze me in their scope and how she translates this ambition into small moments of emotionally devastating language. She doesn't pick one or the other, but goes for, and succeeds in, both. I'm thinking of *Humanimal* and *Schizophrene* specifically, but all her work does this. She also folds performance and even note taking into her writing, which introduces other layers of beautiful, messy complication.

Cynthia Cruz is the all around best writer and kindest human being. Her lines are (often) short, her syntax fragmented, her ideas translated through objects. The result is an almost painful honesty and openness. Her honesty, too, comes through in her portrayal of working class subjects. When she does expand her lines, it's beyond moving. *The Glimmering Room* has a sequence of poems titled "New York State" that observe the lives of institutionalized adolescent girls. These poems have such a powerful effect on me that I'm not equipped to talk about them in any meaningful way, other than to say I cry every time I read them. This crying isn't the result of "trauma porn"—it's because of how Cruz writes about these girls and how much I relate to them/the writing.

Larry Levis, a new poetic obsession of mine, has a similar openness and honesty. He has a sequence titled "The Perfection of Solitude" in *The Widening Spell of the Leaves* that's had a profound effect on my mind, spirit, and poems. These poems are similar to Bhanu Kapil's in scope. Levis moves from Oaxaca to Denver to all around California to so many other places. He ends up in metaphysical spaces, inhabiting paintings and other works of art, while never straying from strange and deft observations. My current favorite line of poetry is from the end of the fourth poem in the sequence—"Cloudy, & not necessarily human." He's describing a dead horse's eye, but also manages to capture how I feel most days.

John Murillo is the unquestionable patron saint of contemporary American poetry. He and Cruz are both Levis fans, so I'm noticing a through line here. I think of Murillo as a confessional poet, not afraid to bear the personal and ugly (or purposeful and messy). Through doing this, he makes the personal and ugly into the universal and beautiful. He'll then move beyond the "confessional mode" to something like humor or a crown of persona sonnets about a teenager who killed cops. I can't. We don't deserve him.

As an editor, I get to see a lot of writing trends ebb and flow out of popularity; right now, one of the biggest seems to be an all-or-nothing approach to punctuation. I read a lot of submissions with either grammatically 'correct' punctuation usage and others with almost all the punctuation omitted. While I don't think either choice is inherently better than the other, I do appreciate a collection like yours that takes the tricky middle-ground of addressing punctuation on a poem-by-poem basis. How do you approach punctuation in your poems? What parts of punctuation feel vital to your writing? Inversely, what guides you in deciding to go with no punctuation in a poem?

It's so funny you ask this. I've been wondering the same thing, and asking these questions of myself and others, throughout my graduate school experience. Very little punctuation is what I'm seeing the most of right now. I'd also add, like you did, that neither is good or bad. I love an unpunctuated poem as much as the next person. I let the flow of language and rhythm in a particular fragment, line, idea, sentence, stanza guide me. That's a somewhat disingenuous answer because "flow" contains within it things like syntax, diction, even rhetoric. All of these bring with them their own considerations. Still, I find myself almost always going with what feels right. I should also note I'm a pretty bad punctuationist. So my reliance on rhythm was really born of insecurity and uncertainty. As for choosing no punctuation, I think it has something to do with the weight of the language. Poems that use nouns in a weird, de-familiar way, those which use a clipped or fragmented sentence structure, those which intentionally disregard or play with syntax—these usually feel like they don't need punctuation. The language itself can dictate how the reader moves through, understands, and experiences the poem. This gestures back towards syntax, so I'm afraid I've repeated myself. Somewhat prosaically, whoever I'm reading while writing a particular poem has a large impact on punctuation and formal decisions.

Conveying language as a density and mass is such a wonderful

explanation and reveals a lot about the structures in this collection. When reading your poems, the feeling is something akin to standing on a bridge, with each new word or piece of punctuation adding more and more weight. That sense of potential collapse that comes through in your syntax and spacing has the dual effect of being tense and mesmerizing; it feels similar to some of Anne Sexton's more climactic poems. What would your advice be for poets looking to gain greater control over their syntax and punctuation usage? Inversely, did you receive any advice that proved less than useful?

Oh wow, thank you for those incredibly kind words! I didn't mention her above, but Anne Sexton is another big influence when it comes to honesty. How could she not be? She also wins the award for best book title for *The Awful Rowing Toward God*. I'm not sure if I have specific advice for poets other than to read. Read poetry, of course, but also fiction and nonfiction. Read fiction that traffics in beautiful sentences and then fiction that's plot-and-pacing-based. Read biography, memoir, craft books, and reviews. Read theory and frustratingly dense academic texts. These often have the most convoluted syntax and can be read as poems (which also removes some of the pressure to understand their Big Ideas). So, read theory for language, syntax, and rhythm. After you've read enough that you want to vomit, talk about it with fellow language nerds. This can be in a workshop or seminar setting, but have you ever called up a friend to geek out over a poet's punctuation? It's kind of wonderful. All of this reading will make your writing so much messier (there's that word again) at first, but it'll also lead you into really exciting and interesting uses of language.

There really is something special about messiness in writing, and how much more so in our poetry's visual language. I like your answer here, because it contextualizes so much of why we tell young poets to read voraciously, to build out that writing toolbox with any implement you could ever need. Did your own reading habits come naturally or was there a catalyst? Even more specifically, do you remember any of the reading inspirations for this collection of poems?

The act of reading for pleasure was always natural. That's how people become writers, I think—by being bookworms as kids. Whatever critical or active reading habits I have came from grad school. Workshop helped me become a better writer by becoming a more conscious and attuned reader. The after-workshop conversations, too, were so valuable to talking about reading and building reading habits. So, yeah, MFAs are exclusive, gatekeeping, possible pyramid schemes, but I needed one to learn how to read thoroughly and thoughtfully. I have too many reading inspirations for these poems. Two powerful ones were "Some Days in April" coming from Rosemary Mayer's artist book of the same name (you can find it online and it's stunning) and "I don't like to sing about boxing but I hope you'll understand" coming after reading Carol Guess' *Tinderbox Lawn*. Both of these books sent me running to the page.

ACKNOWLEDGEMENTS

Thank you to the editors, readers, designers, and everyone else who brought the following poems into the world for the first time:

"Body by Adderall" *Hayden's Ferry Review*, 2016
"I don't like to sing about boxing but I hope you'll understand"
    New South, 2018
"The first time my father cut himself" *The Southeast Review*, 2019
"Poem for Florida" *BathHouse Journal*, 2020
"An incomplete history of" x2, *DIAGRAM*, 2020
"Palliative on a Rooftop" *Bellevue Literary Review*, 2021
"Skinny Fisted Sons" *Blood Tree Literature*, 2021
"Where are the worms in my mouth brother in your mouth"
    Lillet Press' Splashes, 2021
"A Poem to Pass the Time" excerpted, *Prelude*, 2021
"We the Dead Balk" *Superstition Review*, 2021
"The Body Itself Crude & Chanted" *Denver Quarterly*, 2022

There are too many people to thank. I'll briefly, and inadequately, say:

Thank you to my parents, Cathy and Warren. My grandmother, Mae. My aunt, Lauren. My cousins, aunts, uncles.

Thank you to my friends in Florida. Phil, Ryan, Jason, Sam B, Sam N, Jasper, Daniel. Steve, Jeff, Dennis, all the Olympic Height's guys. My first poetry heroes from Dada's and The Funky Buddha.

Thank you to everyone from UMass Amherst. Peter, Dara, Ocean, Cynthia, Noy, CA, Ruth, Jordy, Jennifer. Your workshops, seminars, and individual guidance created these poems. Molly, Raquel, Emily, Janke. Gremlin and Goblin. Mike, Juleen, Aaron, Eliot, Jade. Joe, Laney, Chris, CJ. Merita, Ty, Ell, Barucha. Emilie, Rebecca, Roman, Amy, Cleo, Leah, Jane, Layne. Everyone from workshop I've inevitably forgotten. These poems wouldn't exist without each of you. The poems remember when I forget.

Thank you Hannah, keeper of the list, most thoughtful reader and note taker, mother of cat dragons, allergy medication goddess, potential bundle of raccoons in a human suit. There aren't enough superlatives.

Thank you to everyone at USM. You're pushing my poems in strange and exciting directions.

Thank you Jerrod and James. Reijer and Sally. This book is as much yours as mine.

Thank you to the writers, artists, and human beings who inspired, in large part and small, the following poems:

"Some Days in April" takes its title from, and is after, Rosemary Mayer.

"Where are the worms in my mouth brother in your mouth" is after Bhanu Kapil.

"I don't like to sing about boxing but I hope you'll understand" take its title from the band *This Bike is a Pipe Bomb* and owes a debt to Carol Guess.

"A Poem to Pass the Time" was written after a number of soma(atic) poetry rituals performed with CA Conrad, Mike Medeiros, Juleen Johnson, JL Lapinel, Laura S. Marshall, Marcella Haddad, Sarah Coates, and Jamie Thomson

David Greenspan is a PhD candidate at the University of Southern Mississippi. He earned an MFA in Poetry from UMass Amherst. This is his first book.

CPSIA information can be obtained
at www.ICGtesting.com
Printed in the USA
LVHW030459070222
709998LV00003B/12

9 781949 065152